MW01089269

Morel Mushrooms
In Michigan

And Other Great Lakes States

By Vic Eichler, Ph.D.

Pen & ink drawings by Marianne Ruth Beard

ISBN: 978-0-9703620-5-6

Manufactured in the United States of America
Copyright © 2010 by Victor B. Eichler

All rights reserved under International and Pan-American copyright conventions.
No part of this book may be reproduced, stored in a retrieval system, or
transmitted in any form, electronic, mechanical, or by other means, without
written permission of the author.

Cover layout by Julie Taylor.

Shantimira Press
P.O. Box 171
Three Rivers, MI 49093-0171

shantimirapress@yahoo.com

Morel mushrooms will suddenly appear
When oak leaves are the size of a mouse's ear
North American Folklore

DEDICATION

This small volume is dedicated to Joe Breidenstein of Walloon Lake who passed away in 2009. Joe had a passion for promoting tourism in Michigan and he was a great supporter of anything dealing with morels. He created two outings well-known to shroomers: "Morels & More" and "Fall Mushroom Mania" in order to spread his love of morels and to popularize the joys of finding and preparing wild Michigan mushrooms. He co-created and coordinated the "Chef's Challenge" with his friend Rick Coates which also helped to popularize a variety of springtime culinary activities including the preparation of morels as a gourmet treat. Joe was a most giving person whose memory will be honored by all who knew him.

*

Also, to Ruth, partner on the path of discovery. I enjoy the memory of your first delightful taste of a wild morel!

TABLE OF CONTENTS

I. INTRODUCTION

This book was the result of two fortuitous meetings. First, in the Spring of 2009, the author and his wife had the good fortune of staying several nights at the Jordan Inn, located in East Jordan, Michigan, at the very end of morel season in the area. At that time, they learned that the resident chef, Joseph Krumholtz, was well-known throughout the northern part of Michigan's lower peninsula as a superb chef and caterer.

Recognizing that the 49th Annual Morel Festival in nearby Boyne City was now history meant that the following Spring – 2010 – the area would be celebrating the 50th anniversary of this national event. We talked about creating a book to be published by my publishing company that included a variety of recipes that Joseph would contribute to commemorate this historic milestone.

The second fortuitous meeting occurred in the village of Constantine, only a few miles from the Indiana border in southern Michigan. The author was introduced to Marianne Ruth Beard, a most gifted and talented young artist, who lives and goes to school in Colorado when not visiting in Michigan.

Marianne enjoys sketching from nature, and she accepted the challenge to illustrate this book to clearly define the differences between the three varieties of morel mushrooms in both surface view and in logitudinal section. The accompanying drawings illustrate better than photographs the defining characteristics of each variety and are truly a feast for the eyes so that you – the morel hunter who is reading this book - can have a morel feast safely and enjoyably at the table.

Shroomer (noun) – *(1) any of a variety of hunter/gatherers of wild mushrooms for either the fun of the hunt or an addiction to their taste. (2) a crazed individual who seeks excitement in finding mushrooms in the wild, especially the edible variety. (3) A man, woman or child who, when asked where they find wild mushrooms, will never tell a lie, but who may really stretch the truth!*

II. WHY THIS BOOK?

With a number of useful guides to hunting morel mushrooms a reader might ask, "Why another book?" The answer is, "It fills a need!" Many of the books that exist on locating and harvesting this gastronomic treasure are: (1) more academic than a "shroomer" might need (do you really need to read about ongoing DNA analysis of various varieties?), (2) far too global for the Midwestern hunter, (3) filled with excessive discussion of dangers one might encounter in the field, or (4) complicated in the discussion of variables which might exist.

This volume is dedicated to a clear and simple explanation of what a morel mushroom hunter in Michigan (and adjacent Great Lakes states) needs to know without oversimplifying the information or failing to include basics for the beginner as well as for the advanced morel hunter.

Of the more than 2,000 varieties of mushrooms that inhabit the Great Lakes states, only a few are edible; many more are to be avoided due to chemicals they produce which can cause symptoms from headaches and nausea to coma and death. It is therefore of utmost importance to be able to distinguish the edible varieties from those that must be avoided. Our focus here will be on the several morphological varieties (which may actually be different, but related, species) that are 'lumped into' the generic name: "Morels."

It is important to note at the onset that there is tremendous variability regarding where, when, and why morels are found anywhere. In Chapter VI, many of these variables are explored. However, all experienced shroomers know that the "truth" that is shared among colleagues is rarely "the whole truth, and nothing but the truth." After all, sharing information about the location of a fine collecting place for hundreds of morels would only bring others to the collection site, and that is information to be protected – even among good friends and family! It's a popular story, told in jest by an experienced shroomer to a neophyte, "Sure I can tell you where I found these beauties . . . but then I'd have to shoot you!"

III. The Basics to Distinguish Morels

There are two basic constructions of a mushroom: either it has the traditional cap, and lined with gills below (where the spores form) resting on a lower stalk, or it lacks the 'umbrella-like' cap and has a spongy appearance (the 'fruiting body') around the upper part of the stalk. The latter is the structure of the morel mushroom.

However, there are mushrooms, called 'False Morels' which also have a more-or-less spongy appearance to the fruiting body. A discussion of the various species of false morels is beyond the scope of this book; however, detailed descriptions and photos of these mushrooms can be found in field guides and on the Internet. Let it be sufficient here to mention one feature that can distinguish between the true morels (genus *Morchella*) and the false pretenders (genus *Verpa* and genus *Gyromitra*, for example) is that the inside of the cap and the stem of the true morels are HOLLOW, while the inside of the stem, and usually also the cap, of the false morels are NOT HOLLOW. A valuable rhyme states: "If the mushroom is not hollow, you must not swallow." In addition, the bottom edge of the cap of the true morel is attached to the bottom of the stalk, while the bottom edge of the cap of a false morel generally hangs free of the stalk.

It cannot be emphasized enough that a person must know what kind of mushroom he is putting in his mouth, as mushrooms – by their very nature – possess toxins that can cause (at the very least) gastric distress in sensitive persons. Some species of mushrooms possess toxins that are truly lethal, although it is not likely that the morel hunter will mistake these for the object of their search. It is advised that a novice morel hunter pair up with an experienced shroomer when the spring hunting season arrives, or at least have an experienced person identify your finds before cooking, preserving or eating them fresh.

Distinguishing the Common Types of Morels

True morels are found with two basic shapes and in two basic colors (of which there are gradations of color frequently encountered). One characteristic that all of the true morels share is that they are hollow inside the cap and the stem. This is a critical thing to note to distinguish them from other mushrooms that may have an outward appearance that resembles the "true morels." Some mushrooms called "false morels" may have a cap with ridges attached at the top of the stem, but the stem will either be solid or filled with a fibrous material.

Two Basic Shapes of Morels

The two basic shapes of the "True Morels" are: a) the full cap, and b) the half-free cap and are distinguished as follows.

The Full Cap Morels:

The first morels to appear are generally up to five inches tall, with a spongy appearing cap that sits above and is firmly attached at the bottom to the short stem (also called stalk or stipe) which is an inch or more long. The spongy fruiting body consists of ridges around vertical-oriented pits within which the spores form. The upper tip of the elongated fruiting body may be rounded or pointed, and the ridges generally appear lighter than the inside of the pits. The cap is fused along its length with the stalk. This structure is typical of the light colored morels and the dark morels which are distinguished below by general color and time of appearance during the morel season.

Typical 'Full Cap' morel in surface view and longitudinal section. Note the attachment of the bottom of the cap to the stem in the right-hand drawing.

The Half-Free Cap Morels:

This variety of morel is distinguished, as the name implies, by the unique attachment of the fruiting body to the stem. It is classified as *Morchella semilibera*, which means "morel that is partly free" (of the stem). The fruiting body is quite short, attached at the very top of a stem which may be four to five (or more) times the length of the cap. When seen in section, the cap is partly attached to the stem, attached only at the top half while the lower half of the cap hangs free from the stem.

The half-free morels are generally not as well-known as the full cap morels, for their appearance in any season is hard to predict. It has been reported that in some years they are present in large numbers, while in other years they won't be found at all. There appears to be no apparent cycle in which years they are numerous or just what triggers their presence. That remains to be deciphered.

The Half-Free morel, Morchella semilibra. Note that the lower edge of the cap is not fused with the stem in the longitudinal section, at right

Photograph of Half-Free Cap Morels

Two Basic Colors of Morels

Besides distinguishing these wild delicacies by shape, the full cap morels are also referred to by the predominant color of their fruiting body. These are possibly variations of the same species, although some authors give them separate species designations.

Many mycologists are involved in elucidating the relationships, even doing DNA analyses to distinguish their relationships. Some taxonomists have suggested there are as few as three or four distinct species, others suggest the number of distinct species number in the dozens.

The Peterson Field Guide to Mushrooms of North America by McKnight & McKnight lists the following Morels: *Morchella esculenta* (the Common Morel), *M. angusticeps* (Narrowhead Morel), *M. conica* (Black Morel). *M. crassipes* (Thick-Footed Morel), *M. atrotomntosa* (Burnsite Morel) and *M. semilibera* (Half-Free Morel). We avoid use of distinct species names for the morels, however, except for the morphologically distinct Half-Free Morels since there is no consistent agreement on the species names, at least by color. Let it suffice here to just understand that the morels described here are all considered to be in the same genus: *Morchella* (from the old German word 'morchel', for 'mushroom').

The "Black Morels"

The so-called "black morels" typically are the first ones to appear. The black morels actually appear in various shades from black to dark brown to dark tan. They arrive first among the morels as the main season approaches. The pits appear lighter than the ridges in young mushrooms, but darken to appear the same color as the ridges as the fungus is exposed to light. Regardless of the degree of darkness, the mushroom is seen to have a shallow indented rim around the stem at the point of attachment of the cap, which is unlike the lighter varieties.

A black morel as found in nature

12

The black morel (left) and its appearance in section (right)

The "Yellow Morels"

The yellow morels are found with fruiting bodies whose ridges vary from white to gray to yellow. The pits may be dark in a young specimen, but lighten as they age. In a typical season they will be found a few weeks after the first of the black morels are collected, although they may overlap for a few weeks, depending on the location and environmental conditions. In some communities, these variations in colors are determined to be separate varieties; in others they are considered just to be different seasonal or growth stage differences in color of the same species.

A small group of yellow morel; see also color photo on front cover

IV. FUNGI - WHAT WE KNOW ABOUT THEM

Fungi (plural of fungus) are multicellular organisms that are considered distinct from plants and animals, while having characteristics of both. Like both plants and animals, the fungus organism has true cells, containing nuclei that are bound within a membrane and contain chromosomes. The cells of fungi possess a cellulose cell wall characteristic of plants and unlike the cells of animals; however, fungi cells lack the green pigment chlorophyll, and thus the ability to photosynthesize their own food from the sun's energy, making them similar to animal cells in this regard.

In the absence of chlorophyll and the ability to make their own food, fungi must obtain their essential nutrients from other living organisms. They are therefore either **parasitic** (obtaining their food from living plants or animals), **saprobes** (obtaining nutrients from non-living, decomposed organisms) or **symbionts** (living in a close and mutually beneficial partnership with a different species of organism).

Morels happen to be saprobes, and therefore they are found where they grow best – around dead, decaying and decomposing leaves, trees, or other plants. That is why emphasis in a later chapter is given to OLD orchards, or the remains of forests AFTER a fire has killed many of the burned trees. These conditions facilitate the development of the morels. Various species of fungi are found around the world – in a great diversity of habitats – ranging from deserts to deep ocean environments. They, along with bacteria, are the primary decomposers of organic material on the earth. In this capacity they are indispensable in the process called "nutrient cycling," in which they break down organic nutrients to forms other organisms can use for their own life purposes.

Besides providing a gourmet addition to a meal – such as morels and other edible mushrooms - fungi have a long association with humans in a variety of ways. Briefly, some of the useful ways we benefit from fungi include those known as yeasts which are used in the fermentation process in making beer and wine, and 'Baker's yeast' used in the rising of bread. The discovery of penicillin and cephalosporin from fungus molds created the antibiotic industry, and these and other drugs made from fungi are used in numerous therapies and chemotherapies at the present time. Specific species of molds are used to make sauces, such as soy sauce, and some cheeses, such as Roquefort and other 'blue' cheeses, incorporate molds in their production.

Not all fungi benefit humans, though. Many diseases of food crops, such as rusts, ergots and smuts cause tremendous damage if allowed to spread in mono-cultured fields. Some common diseases or ailments associated with fungi in humans are ringworm of the scalp, athlete's foot between the toes, and yeast infections of mucous membranes of the body. Fortunately, none of these ailments would ever be caused by, or confused with, morel mushrooms!

V. Morel Growth Cycle

Morel mushrooms, like other fungi, begin their life cycle as spores that are released from the cap of a mature individual. The spongy-looking cap of the morel is known as the "fruiting body," a complex structure which disperses spores formed within.

The spores are often carried by the wind to a distant site where, if the substrate is suitable for growth, the spore begins to produce a network of thin filaments called hypha. The hypha quickly grow, feeding on decaying plant material in the soil, and branch to form a network called 'mycelia' (plural of 'mycelium'). These mycelia rapidly grow into the food source and, in time, small colonies of cells begin to organize within them. This "hyphal knot" is the first indication of an organized future mushroom body.

A tiny stalk develops in the ground and forms a tiny knob-like cap. The hyphae lie dormant during dry periods, but after a brief spring rain they are stimulated to swell and elongate, pushing the cap through the fallen leaves which often lie above the developing mushroom. This can happen incredibly fast, becoming obvious in the morning after none was seen the day before.

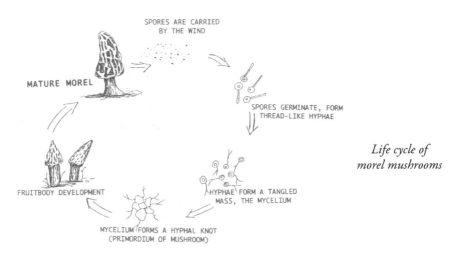

SPORES ARE CARRIED BY THE WIND

MATURE MOREL

SPORES GERMINATE, FORM THREAD-LIKE HYPHAE

FRUITBODY DEVELOPMENT

HYPHAE FORM A TANGLED MASS, THE MYCELIUM

MYCELIUM FORMS A HYPHAL KNOT (PRIMORDIUM OF MUSHROOM)

Life cycle of morel mushrooms

VI. Variables of the Hunt

Morel hunting season in Michigan (and other Great Lakes states) may extend from mid-April to the end of June, with some variability due to other climatic (humidity, temperature and sunlight), environmental (terrain, geography, soil type, recent burnings, forest cover) and biological factors. These will be considered in detail below. The earlier dates refer more particularly to the southern states of the Great Lakes region (Illinois, Indiana and Ohio). As one goes further north in Michigan, Wisconsin and Minnesota, and the more eastern states of Pennsylvania and New York, the expected beginning of "the season" would be later. The reader is advised to check the updated activity of the season by state on the morel message boards located on the web at *www.morels.com*. Join in the discussions and contribute to your own seasonal experiences!

Climate

Humidity

Mushrooms, like other spring plants, respond to the melting of snow and early spring rains to germinate. The spring of 2009 was one of the wettest on record in the Great Lakes states; rivers overflowed their banks, ponds consolidated to become lakes, and the profuseness of flowers, fruits and berries of all kinds were obvious. It was also a banner year for morel mushrooms! Moisture in the air and in the soil is a key ingredient in determining the beginning of shroomer season. Looking around wooded areas and underbrush, as well as along stream beds the morning after a night's rain, are good places to hunt for morels.

Temperature

Air and ground temperature have an apparent impact on the growing cycle, with a minimum 'trigger' temperature that seems lower for the early black morels and a bit higher (and thus a week or two later in the spring) for the yellow morels. The approximate range for daytime temperatures is mid-50s to mid-70s degrees Fahrenheit, and the range for nighttime temperatures is approximately 40-50 degrees Fahrenheit. A hot, moist day which is followed by several cool days and nights, appears to be a suitable 'trigger' for the initiation of development of morels. However, cycles vary from year to year, causing variation in this description of the influence of temperature.

Sunlight

Morels are found away from sunlight, in ground shaded by trees, especially hardwoods. Although sunlight provides warmth to the air and ground, direct sunlight will dry the soils that are important to the growth of morels. Therefore, seek sites that are at least mostly or entirely out of direct sunlight.

Environment

Terrain

Morels are found just about anywhere; that is part of the reason that the hunt for them is so enticing. The early black morels seem to favor drier areas than the yellow morels – hardwood or mixed forests, hilltop areas and even along gravel roads. The yellow morels are more likely to be found in bottomland where the soil is richer and more likely to be moist. Both can be numerous once they break through the overlying leaf cover. When the expected season begins, the earliest morels are likely to be found on the south-facing hillsides where the sun warms the soil earliest.

Geography

There is a definite south to north movement of the season with morels found earlier in the southern counties of the state and later as one goes north. In Michigan, the hunt generally begins as early as mid-April in southern Michigan and may continue until mid-June in the north.

Soil Type

Since the development of morels depends on nutrients found in the soil, the best type of soil to find them in is moist and high in organic matter. Such soil facilitates the transfer of nutrients to the growing mushroom. Decayed leaf litter in hardwood forests is one source of organic matter useable by morels.

Recent Burnings

Many collectors have remarked about the prevalence of large groups of spring morels in areas that have been burned in the previous year. After a forest fire, for example, abundant crops will be found for several years. Why burned trees and soil triggers the growth of mushrooms is not known for sure. Perhaps burned trees release minerals which are desirable for mushroom growth. Another possibility is that the soil is warmed by the increase in sunlight in the absence of the canopy of trees that were formerly shading the area.

Biological Associations

It would be difficult to try to persuade a veteran shroomer that there is no clear association between morels and a particular variety of tree. Morel hunters "know" from experience that they will find most of their bounty under a particular species of tree. "Always have; always will!" they say. However, even though there has never been a proven symbiotic mycorrhizal relationship between the mushrooms and even one species of tree, various hunters swear that the ground under their favorite species will yield the majority of quarry for the day.

The most common trees named as the best 'hunting ground' are the ash, elm, and apple trees. The next tier of favorites would include aspens, sycamore, tulip trees, poplar and cottonwood trees. No doubt any old timer who reads this would argue that some other species will yield the bulk of treasured morels – and so we feel it best to let experience be your best guide.

There is some humor in listening to arguments about the best tree species under which the most morels are found. One shroomer might argue that there is no doubt that dying elm trees will yield the most mushrooms, only to be countered by his friend arguing that if that is so, the largest morels are sure to be found in a grove of ash trees!

There are many reports that dead or dying apple trees – the remains of an old deserted orchard, perhaps – is favored over healthy apple trees. That is the author's experience as well. For some reason not understood, dying trees appear to be a richer environment for the mycelia to persist and grow. This was also the experience in the late 1950s in the Midwest when Dutch Elm Disease was rampant, destroying large numbers of susceptible elm trees. For many years later, large populations of morels were reported around dying elm trees.

VII. Practical Considerations

Preparing for the Hunt

The 'Number One" consideration for mushroom hunting is to respect private property! Whether hunting mushrooms, wild turkey, or white-tail deer, the same courtesy applies. To hunt where you do not have permission is trespassing, and rural folks do not take kindly to trespassing whether trees or fences along the property lines are marked or not. What remains is either to hunt on your own land, to obtain permission from a rural landowner to hunt on his property, or to confine your morel hunting to a public park or state recreational or wildlife management area that allows mushrooming. Public wildlife management areas are different than areas dedicated as a nature preserve. The latter, without exception, will not allow disruption or removal of any plant, animal, rock or soil!

Besides dressing appropriately for the cool spring weather in situations where you want to remain dry as you traverse the terrain, there are a few suggestions that are appropriate for the shroomer during the field collecting trip. Long pants are important if you will be hunting in areas where overgrowths of wild multiflora roses, berry bushes with thorns, or poison ivy reside. These are often common in old orchards that have been abandoned. If the weather looks like rain may occur during the time you are in the field, a light raincoat and waterproof boots or shoes are, of course, sensible items for the day.

Whether the terrain is flat or hilly, experienced hikers know that a walking stick is a valuable tool to take on the walk. In addition, the mushroom hunter may find it useful in many regards: to turn over leaves which may be hiding mushrooms beneath without having to bend down to investigate, to give balance as you climb hills, to tap 'bumps' in the ground to test if there are rocks (which might be slippery underfoot) or perhaps to check if small groups of morels lie beneath.

The author is not personally bothered by mosquitoes, but for those who are, a mosquito repellant may be necessary. I prefer to wear a hat with a neckerchief protecting the back of my neck, and a long sleeve shirt to cover my arms. However, long sleeves add to the temperature one feels as one walks up, down and over the land, so carrying ample drinking water is encouraged to help you keep cool and replenish the moisture you might lose to perspiration.

If you are walking in unfamiliar territory - especially in a large state recreation area, for example - a compass (and knowledge about how to use it) may be something you want to be sure you take with you so you can find yourself "out of the woods." Alternatively, if you own a portable 'global positioning system' (GPS), this will aid you in returning to your parked vehicle. Take care not to leave cleared or marked trails for any distance as you hunt for morels. Your eyes will be watching the ground, and many shroomers have found that the way back is not as easy to find when not paying attention to where he or she is walking into a woods away from a trail!

Collecting morels

While serious shroomers like to keep their 'hunting grounds' to themselves, it is often sensible to cultivate a hunting buddy if you explore areas that are otherwise unknown to you – or to make the hunt a family affair to share the joy of morel hunting with family members! There is a need to be aware of safety when exploring new land, or even previously explored land, and there is no substitute for having someone who can assist if one gets in unexpected trouble - such as spraining an ankle, slipping on a wet rock, encountering one of the several species of rattlesnakes that may just have ventured out from its winter burrow, etc.

One of the biggest dangers you might encounter in the spring if you explore public hunting grounds is being mistaken (by sound) for a herd of wild turkeys by a turkey hunter who is occupying the same woods as you are. This is a danger that has been written about by many authors; such an idea may bring smiles to a reader, but has, in fact, endangered more than one mushroom hunter.

Two sensible additions to carry are a sharp folding knife and a small skein of nylon rope. They may come in handy in a variety of situations. A cell phone (alternatively a whistle) would be useful if hunting alone and you need to contact help or signal anyone who might be in the vicinity.

Only a novice hunter of morels will pull the quarry from the ground; this is a collecting method to be avoided at all costs! Pulling the mycelium – which are likened to the roots of a plant – out of the ground will cause damage and will prevent the fungus from forming another fruiting body later in the season or in the future. The fruiting body MUST be cut with a knife just above the ground for two reasons: 1) it will preserve the mycelelium in the ground from being harmed, and 2) cutting the stalk will avoid putting extra sand or dirt in your collecting bag which will otherwise need to be cleaned from the morels before eating.

Experienced shroomers know that a netted bag – such that onions are packaged for sale - is necessary for collecting morels for several reasons. This allows the spores of the morels to scatter from the bag and hopefully land in soil which will perpetuate the species for the next season. Also, the mesh allows air to pass over the morels to keep them fresh and cool, something that collecting in either a paper or plastic bag will not provide.

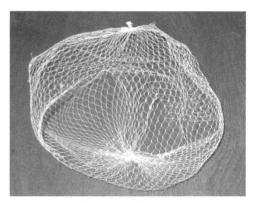

A netted bag for collecting morels

Leave morels with soft or mushy caps; they will not give you the enjoyment of younger specimens; also, leave those that look old and wormy. Again, you can do better elsewhere.

The aftermath of a successful hunt!

VIII. Enjoying the Fruits of Your Labors

Preserving mushrooms

This chapter will not be of concern to you unless you are fortunate to have an oversupply of the tasty morsels. There is such joy in eating wild morels fresh that unless you have morels in surplus, you will want to cook them your favorite way. However, the day may come when you do have mushrooms in excess of what you and your family or friends can eat immediately, and the following methods are tried and true ways to preserve them.

In any of the methods described below it is wise to first clean the external surface and the pits of the morels to remove plant debris, sand or insects (or an occasional slug, snail or beetle that may be present) before progressing. Then, for each method it is desirable to slice the mushrooms longitudinally to check that the inside is not harboring any dirt or living organisms. Then, without washing, select one of the following methods to preserve. Soaking morels removes their unique flavor very quickly. Remember that it is necessary to cook preserved mushrooms before eating!

Dehydrating
Drying mushrooms is a popular way to preserve your oversupply of morels. The least expensive way to remove water from morels is to string them on a thin string (with a button or similar object at the bottom) and hang them in a warm, dry place. It is best that warm air moves across the string of morels to aid in drying them. A variety of commercial electric dehydrators are available, or an inexpensive one can be made with a light bulb for heat and a small fan to blow the heat over the screen trays that fit inside a heated box. Since mushrooms have a high degree of water in their tissues they will shrink tremendously and therefore a large number will be reduced into a small volume. By slicing the morels lengthwise you will allow the trapped moisture to exit the tissue more rapidly, thereby reducing dehydration time.

One note: be sure to dehydrate completely or mold may develop. Store in a zip lock bag (with as much air removed as possible) or in a glass jar with good

An example of an electronic dehydrator

seal or, better yet, seal in a vacuum pack which will allow the dried mushroom to remain good for years. Dehydrated mushrooms may be used in salads dried, or rehydrated in hot water for five to ten minutes (or cool water, milk or wine for one-half hour) and cooked as you would freshly picked. The rehydrated morels will retain the fresh flavor and aroma, even after being stored dry for a year or more. Since morels are approximately 75% water, when a recipe calls for 8 oz. of fresh morels use 2 oz. of dried mushrooms rehydrated. The flavor will be as good, perhaps even enhanced, after rehydrating.

Freezing

Freezing is an excellent way to preserve extra mushrooms for later use. Without washing, place the dry, cleaned morels in a frying pan to sauté completely in melted butter. Allow to cool and then store the halves with the associated juice in plastic freezer bags or containers before placing in the freezer. To avoid a tough or 'rubbery' texture, cook frozen morels without first thawing by putting the frozen pieces directly into a hot frying pan on medium to medium-high heat.

Canning

Canning is a third method that might be used by individuals who regularly 'put up' fruits or vegetables and are experienced with the method. It is of great importance that a person who cans mushrooms have a pressure cooker with a good seal. The high heat required to insure that any bacterial contaminants are destroyed may reduce the beneficial nutrient value of the mushrooms, but with the right equipment and available jars this method can preserve morels satisfactorily.

Nutrition Information

Mushrooms, in general, provide high levels of essential and desirable nutrients. Data available are not specific to wild morel mushrooms, but rather are obtained from popular store-bought varieties such as portabello, crimini, shitakes and white button mushrooms.

Nevertheless, data indicate that mushrooms are a rich source of antioxidants including three essential B-vitamins (riboflavin, niacin and pantothenic acid), plus folate and the essential minerals copper, selenium, potassium, iron, phosphorus, manganese and zinc. They are high in fiber and a rich source of potassium, both of which assist in keeping our bodies in good health. Moreover, they are low in sodium, low in calories (about 20 calories per cupful) and are free of fat and cholesterol.

The high level of nutrients are considered to be protective against several forms of disease; selenium is believed to be active in protecting against prostate cancer, and mushrooms added to meals are being studied in several anti-cancer and anti-diabetic diets as well as immunity-strengthening regimes. Research studies have shown that white button mushrooms in the diet may increase the body's immunity to viral infections and tumors by increasing activity levels of compounds important for our acquired as well as inborn immunity.

The National Institutes of Health, along with the California Breast Cancer Research Program and the American Institute for Cancer Research, are involved in clinical trials at research hospitals looking for relationships between mushrooms in the diet and diabetes, cancer and other catastrophic illnesses. The national Mushroom Council has contributed support to the early clinical trials. Already published research results are encouraging that compounds found naturally in mushrooms enhance natural killer cell activity in the body which in turn may reduce the size of cancer tumors and play a role in preventing cancers.

IX. CHEF JOSEPH KRUMHOLZ'S MOREL RECIPES

There are many sites on the Internet where wonderful recipes for morel mushrooms can be found, and the reader is encouraged to refer to them for basic methods to prepare mushrooms, in general, or morel mushrooms, in particular. Below, we present some gourmet recipes prepared by Chef Krumholz especially for this book.

Like any fine art or science, gourmet cooking has a vocabulary which may have terms unfamiliar to the casual cook. Defined below are a few terms that Chef Krumholz uses in some of his recipes which follow:

Sauté – to cook food quickly and lightly in a little butter or oil

Roux - a mixture of flour and fat that is cooked briefly and used as the thickening base for a soup or sauce

Here are some of Chef Krumholz's favorite ways to prepare morels for his guests. Enjoy!

Chef's 'Quick & Simple' Prep for Morels

INGREDIENTS:

Fresh morels, halved lengthwise; soaked in salt water to remove bugs and debris

Flour to cover

Butter

PROCEDURE:

Melt butter in a non-stick pan over medium heat; pat cleaned morel pieces dry with paper toweling, then dust with flour and sauté. When golden brown turn over.   Enjoy the flavor of these delicious morsels as Nature intended.

Because not all wild mushrooms are safe to eat it is wise – and recommended – that inexperienced mushroom hunters check with a knowledgeable person who has found and identified morel mushrooms before assuming that any particular mushroom is safe to eat. Even when properly prepared some edible mushrooms can cause a reaction in sensitive individuals; a person who is particularly sensitive to any food, including edible mushrooms, should refrain from eating that food.

Morel Infused Olive Oil

This is a very simple recipe with only two components, but it is what you do with the oil that makes it spectacular.

INGREDIENTS:
1 ounce of dried morel mushrooms
2 cups of olive oil

PROCEDURE:
Submerge mushrooms in warm water, then drain thoroughly. Pat dry. Place morels and oil in saucepan and cook over low hear until oil reaches 200 degrees F. Remove from heat, then cover; let stand four hours, then refrigerate. Refrigerated this will have a one month shelf life

USE:
Coat bread squares with the oil and toast to make croutons for salads; try the oil tossed in popcorn, or add a few drops to garnish a cream soup like onion or celery. Possibilities are endless.

Morel Bisque

INGREDIENTS:
1 quart chicken broth
1 pound coarse chopped Morels
1 medium onion coarsely chopped
1/4 pound (one stick) of butter
2 cups heavy cream
Kosher salt and coarse ground black pepper

PROCEDURE:
In a saucepan sauté morels and onion in butter. When the onions become translucent add chicken broth and purée. Add heavy cream then simmer, whisking occasionally. Salt and pepper to taste. Serve immediately.

Morel Maple Dijon Mustard

INGREDIENTS:

1 large fine minced onion
3 cloves fine minced garlic
1 cup fine minced morels
4 ounces dry mustard
2 cups white wine
4 tablespoons of maple syrup
1 tablespoon vegetable oil
2 teaspoons of kosher salt

PROCEDURE:

Combine garlic, onion, and morels in wine and bring to boiling, add additional ingredients mix until smooth.

Morel Mushroom Gravy

This is a great accompaniment for beef, venison, or any red meat roast.

INGREDIENTS:

2 cups thin sliced morels
1/4 cup minced onion
1/4 lb of butter
1 ounce red wine
1/2 cup vegetable stock
1/2 cup water
1 tablespoon flour

PROCEDURE:

Sauté mushrooms and onions in half of the butter. Add red wine and vegetable stock and simmer for twenty minutes. Then melt second half of butter and flour and create a roux in a second sauce pan. Add vegetable and liquid mixture to roux slowly, stirring constantly. If gravy is too thick slowly add water. Salt and pepper to taste before serving.

Morel Omelet

INGREDIENTS:
1/4 cup (or more) of sliced morels
1 tablespoon butter or oil
2 large eggs
1/2 cup of a favorite cheese, shredded
Pinch of salt and black pepper

PROCEDURE:
In a five inch fry pan sauté mushrooms in a liberal amount of butter or oil, then add two beaten eggs; cook each side. Add some of your favorite cheese or slide between two slices of toast for an incredible breakfast sandwich.

Morels and Wild Rice Soup

I prefer to use fresh mushrooms, but if I needed to use dried mushrooms I would add the diced reconstituted morels to the vegetable stock.

INGREDIENTS:
10 cups vegetable stock
1 1/2 cups wild rice
1/2 pound morels sliced
1/2 cup rough chopped carrots
1/2 cup rough chopped onion
1 cup rough chopped celery
1 cup rough chopped cabbage
Salt and pepper

PROCEDURE:
Add wild rice to boiling stock and simmer for ten minutes; add carrots and simmer an additional ten minutes. In olive oil sauté mushrooms, onions, celery and cabbage al dente (the vegetables remaining firm). Marry sautéed vegetables to simmering stock; salt and pepper to taste.

Country Biscuits and Gravy With Morels

INGREDIENTS:
1/2 pound morel mushrooms minced
1/4 pound butter
2 tablespoons cooking oil
1 pint milk
4 tablespoons of flour
Salt and pepper

PROCEDURE:
Sauté mushrooms in melted butter, then remove with slotted spoon when cooked and set aside. Add oil to residual butter in pan then mix flour to create a roux, then add salt and pepper. When roux begins to brown, slowly add milk with a wire wisk. Increase heat and whisk slowly, constantly, until the gravy slowly bubbles; then return morels to pan. Continue stirring until gravy reduces to desired thickness.

Morel Ragout

INGREDIENTS:
3 tablespoons butter
1 tablespoon minced garlic
1/4 cup thin sliced green onion
1 pound sliced Morels
1/2 cup red wine
1 cup chicken stock
3 tablespoons of soy sauce
1 teaspoon of minced fresh thyme
1 teaspoon of minced fresh basil
1 teaspoon of minced fresh oregano
Salt and pepper

PROCEDURE:
Sauté garlic, onion, and mushrooms in butter. Season with salt and pepper. Add wine and reduce liquid to half. Add stock, soy sauce, basil, thyme, and oregano and again reduce liquid to half.

White Wine Morel Cream Sauce

INGREDIENTS:
1/4 pound of butter
1/2 pound of morels
1 tablespoon of garlic
1 cup of cream
1/3 cup of dry white wine

PROCEDURE:
Sauté morels in melted butter, add white wine then simmer two minutes. Add cream and allow to thicken. Salt and pepper to taste

Morel Gnocchi

INGREDIENTS:
3 pounds of peeled and quartered potatoes
1/2 pound of cold minced morel mushrooms sautéed in two tbs. of butter
2 cups of flour
1 egg
1/3 cup finely grated parmesan cheese
1/2 cup minced parsley
Salt and pepper

PROCEDURE:
Cook and thoroughly mash potatoes, then place on a clean cutting board. Create a well in the potatoes and then add the egg to the well and start mixing with a fork. Dust often with flour to absorb moisture. As you are mixing add cheese, parsley, salt and pepper. Work mixture until it has a smooth consistency, then add morels. Knead dough until it does not stick to cutting board but DO NOT OVERWORK DOUGH. Using a pastry bag, pipe out dough in a half to three quarter inch round piping and cut into bite size pieces. Place on parchment paper and make sure they do not stick together. Drop small batches in boiling salted water until they float, then transfer them to ice water to stop cooking. Remove gnocchi from water and coat with olive oil to prevent them from drying out or sticking. Sauté gnocchi in butter for service.

Morel and Basil Pesto

INGREDIENTS:
1 cup morel mushrooms
1 cup toasted pine nuts
1 cup fresh basil
4 cloves chopped garlic
1 cup extra-virgin olive oil
f4 tablespoons lemon juice
Salt and pepper

PROCEDURE:
Combine ingredients and purée, salt and pepper to taste.

Morel Spring Rolls

INGREDIENTS:
1 pound sliced mushrooms
2 cups shredded cabbage
2 grated carrots
1 cup bean sprouts
2 tablespoon extra virgin olive oil
1 tablespoon minced garlic
1 tablespoon hoisin sauce
1 tablespoon oyster sauce
Spring roll wrappers
1 beaten egg
Vegetable oil for frying
Salt and pepper

PROCEDURE:
Sauté garlic, ginger and mushrooms in olive oil. Add carrot and cabbage; cook until cabbage wilts, then remove from heat. Toss mixture with hoisin and oyster sauce, then add bean sprouts and season with salt and pepper. Roll approximately two tablespoons of filling in a wrapper using beaten egg to seal. Deep fry or fry in an inch and a half of 350° oil in frying pan turning until evenly browned.

Morel Mushroom Pierogi

This is the prize winning recipe from 49th Annual Morel Festival.

INGREDIENTS:
Dough
  4 eggs
  1/2 cup milk
  1/2 cup cream
  1/2 cup sour cream
  3/4 teaspoon salt
  1 1/2 teaspoons of baking powder
  4 cups flour

Filling
  2 pounds cooked peeled potatoes
  1/2 pound of minced sautéed morels
  1/4 pound of butter
  Cream

PROCEDURE:
Combine potatoes, morels, and butter and mash, adding cream as needed to achieve a consistent but stiff consistency, then set aside. Combine eggs, milk, cream, sour cream, and salt thoroughly. Add baking powder, and slowly add flour while mixing. Knead the dough until consistent, then continue to add flour until the dough does not stick to your hands. Tear dough chunks and roll into a ball. Press flat - between 1/4-1/2 inch thick. Flour and roll out, flipping occasionally, keeping round, until the dough is 1/16 thick. Cut circle of dough, combine and reuse fall-offs. Place filling in center and fold over; press the edges closed with a fork.

In a pot of boiling water add salt and vegetable or olive oil. Place 8 to 10 pierogi in the pot, stirring gently. Water will return to boil; remove pierogi when they float to top. These pierogi can be coated with oil and saved for later, frozen or eaten now. To eat immediately, sauté in frying pan, browning both sides.

Morel Sausage

INGREDIENTS:

5 pounds ground pork shoulder or rump
1 pound ground morel mushrooms
5 teaspoon kosher salt
3 tablespoon onion powder
3 tablespoon paprika
4 teaspoon sugar
1 tablespoon ground cayenne pepper
2 teaspoon garlic
1/2 cup ice water

PROCEDURE:

Combine all the ingredients thoroughly. Stuff into casings or patty and prepare or add to your favorite recipe

Venison Topped with Morel Mushroom Stroganoff

INGREDIENTS:

1 pound Venison Roast or Steak cut into thin 1 1/2 pieces
1/2 cup of flour
1/3 cup of onion
1/2 pound of morel mushrooms
6 tablespoons butter
1/2 teaspoon tarragon
Salt and pepper
1/2 cup red wine
1 cup sour cream

PROCEDURE:

Dredge meat and brown in three tablespoons of butter; remove from pan and set aside. Sauté onion until they start to become translucent, then add three tablespoons of butter; add mushrooms and continue to sauté approximately four minutes. Add red-wine, tarragon, salt and pepper and return to low simmer. Add meat and sour cream. Serve over rice or noodles.

Morel Ravioli

INGREDIENTS:

Pasta:
  4 whole eggs
  3 egg whites
  Pinch of salt
  3 1/2 cups flour
Filling:
  1/2 pound minced morel mushrooms
  2 tablespoons butter
  2 whole eggs
  1 egg yolk
  1/2 cup ricotta cheese
  1/2 cup finely grated fresh parmesan cheese

PROCEDURE:

Pasta:
Beat three eggs with two egg whites and thoroughly mix with the flour and salt.
Roll dough into two even balls and cover with moist cloth.

Filling:
Sauté mushroom in the melted butter, then remove from heat and add remaining
ingredients (reserving one egg)

To Make the Ravioli:
Roll dough into two thin sheets, shaped like squares. Beat reserved egg and brush
one sheet, then place half-teaspoon of filling spaced two inches apart. Cover first
sheet with filling with the second sheet and press around each mound of filling.
Cut pasta into squares centering between mounds; squares should be two inches
on a side. Cook in boiling salted water with the olive oil. Cooked ravioli will
float. Coating cooked ravioli with olive oil will help prevent sticking.

Famous Morel Mushroom Soufflé

A favorite of Joseph Krumholz and Joe Breidenstein, created by Ruth Mossok Johnston, for Joe Breidenstein's Mushroom Weekends at Walloon Lake, Michigan. A perfect balance of eggs, cheese and the prized morels!

INGREDIENTS:

2 cups fresh or reconstituted morels (cleaned and cut into spirals)
2 1/2 tablespoons of butter or margarine, divided
6 large eggs
1/2 cup heavy whipping cream
1/4 cup freshly grated Parmesan cheese
1/2 teaspoon Dijon mustard
1/2 teaspoon sea salt
1/4 teaspoon white pepper
4 ounces sharp cheddar cheese (shredded)
11 ounces cream cheese, softened

PROCEDURE:

Preheat oven to 375 degrees (rack should be in the middle).
Grease an ovenproof soufflé dish (using 3/4 tablespoon of butter) and set aside.
In a sauté pan, heat the remaining butter until melted and add morel spirals. Sauté mushrooms until cooked (about 3 minutes) and most of the butter is absorbed.

In a blender or food processor fitted with the steel 'S' blade – process eggs, heavy cream, Parmesan cheese, Dijon mustard, salt and pepper, until well blended and smooth.

Add the cheddar cheese and reprocess. Add the cream cheese in small amounts until well blended. Remove cheese mixture to a bowl and stir in the morel mushrooms, mixing thoroughly

Place the soufflé ingredients into the greased oven-proof soufflé dish and bake at 375 degrees for 40-45 minutes or until top is golden brown and springs back when gently tapped with your finger. Remove the soufflé from the oven and serve immediately.

Note: if soufflé seems to brown too quickly, turn heat down slightly.

Morel Crusted Bison Tenderloin
with a Red Wine Demi-Glace

This is the 2010 Chefs Challenge recipe developed by Chef Joseph Krumholz and Chef Craig Coe. The annual Chefs Challenge benefits Challenge Mountain as a celebration of Michigan produce and products. Challenge Mountain is a non-profit organization dedicated to helping the physically impaired, mentally challenged and at-risk youth achieve their maximum potential through adaptive outdoor recreation.

INGREDIENTS:
Great Lakes Buffalo Bison Tenderloin
1 ounce of dried morel mushrooms
1/2 cup of Fustini's Sage and Wild Mushrooms extra virgin olive oil
2 cups of Bison Stock Reduction
1/2 cup of Mackinaw Trail 2007 Cabernet Sauvignon
1/2 cup of thinly sliced morel mushrooms sautéed
Coarse ground pepper, Kosher salt and garlic powder

PROCEDURE:
With a rolling pin, crush dried morels, then sprinkle with salt and pepper. Coat sectioned tenderloin with oil and roll in morel mixture pressing firmly; refrigerate overnight. The day of serving, pan sear tenderloin in olive oil then place in 350 degree preheated oven and cook until tenderloin reaches 120 degree internal temperature. Allow meat to rest at least ten minutes before serving.

Demi-Glace: Reduce wine, then add stock and seasoning. Allow to thicken. Use slurry (water and corn starch) to thicken, adding more as needed. Add mushrooms, slices of tenderloin and Demi-Glace and serve atop redskin mashers aside grilled asparagus.

A bowl of morels ready for the kitchen

X. GREAT LAKES STATES MOREL FESTIVALS & EVENTS

In addition to the long-running and well-known Morel Mushroom Festivals in Michigan, other festivals in Great Lakes states have been organized. Listed here are those that were advertised on the Internet at the time this book was written. For more information on any one of these – and to learn if they are still operating – please check for a listing on the Internet.

Michigan

Mesick, MI

The citizens of Mesick, Michigan have proclaimed their town as the "Mushroom Capital of the World" and began celebrating the local morel mushroom fifty-one years ago (1960). Now, a half-century later the festival, which is sponsored by the Mesick Lions Club, draws thousands of people from all across the nation. The event is a major tourism draw for the area, especially well-attended by mushroom hunters from neighboring states. The festival and related activities are scheduled for the second weekend in May. Contact: *www.mesick-mushroomfest.org*

Boyne City, MI

The 'granddaddy' of the morel mushroom festivals is the 4-day celebration that was begun in 1961, and celebrates it's 50th anniversary in 2010. In addition to the many festival events the popular "Morel Taste of Boyne" is billed as the largest morel mushroom eating event. A highlight of this is the 'Chef's Challenge' in which chefs of area restaurants enter and are judged on their own specialty preparations of the famous fungus. Contact: *www.morelfest.com*

Lewiston, MI

A guided hunt for morels as well as an arts & craft show, mushroom tasting and community exhibits are part of the Lewiston Mushroom Celebration which was held the second weekend of May in this Michigan town. Information about a future celebration can be obtained from the Lewiston Area Chamber of Commerce at: *www.lewistonchamber.com*

Online Resource for Michigan

Check out the Michigan Interactive Morel Mushroom Reports at *www.fishweb. com/recreation/mushrooms/index.html*

Wisconsin

Muscoda, WI

Located a three-hour drive west of Milwaukee, citizens have proclaimed the town as "Wisconsin's Morel Capital" and hold a Morel Mushroom Festival the weekend after Mother's Day each year. Begun in the early 1980's, local attendees collect hundreds of pounds of morels during this festival. Contact: *www.muscoda.com*

Online Resource for Wisconsin

Check out the Wisconsin Morels & Mushrooms Message Board at *www.morels. com/wisconsin*

Illinois

Henry, IL

This small community in northern Illinois was the site of what has been billed as the Illinois State Morel Mushroom Hunting Championship that operated from 1996 to 2008. Held the first Saturday in May, it was begun by Tom and Vicki Nauman of Magnolia, IL The operation was taken over by Tom Davis of Henry, IL who reports that he hopes to continue this event in the future. Contact: *tom@ morelmania.com*. For background information and morel-related products check out the Nauman's Morel Mania website at *www.morelmania.com*

Shelbyville area, IL

"Spores 'n' More Festival" is the name of the event scheduled for the fourth weekend in April in five closely situated towns in rural Illinois. A mushroom hunt and awards ceremony are part of this festival that began in 2004. Contact: *www.lakeshelbyville.com* or the office of tourism in Shelbyville.

Wyoming, IL
The Wyoming Area Chamber of Commerce and the Stark County Economic Development Office began a Morel Mushroom Festival and Auction the first weekend in May, 2009. This event may become an annual event, with mushroom sales, crafts, and other festival events. Contact: *www.starkco.illinois.gov* or *vistaden_60@yahoo.com*.

Online Resource for Illinois
Check out the Illinois Morels & Mushrooms Message Board at *www.morels.com/illinois*

Indiana

Brown County, IN
The Brown County State Park began celebrating an annual Morel Mushroom Festival in 2007 with guided mushroom hunts throughout the park with expert guides leading the hikes. Live music and an arts and crafts fair are an expanded part of the festival, which is celebrated in early May. Contact: *www.browncountys-tatepark.com* or the Brown County State Park Nature Center at 812-988-5240.

Parke County, IN
The Mansfield Village Mushroom Festival in Parke County, Indiana has been enjoyed by mushroom hunters since 1984 and is held the last full weekend in April. It brings in many thousands of visitors to this historic village, and has been expanded to include a Festival Car Show. Contact: *info@mansfieldhilltopfarm.com* or 765-344-1889.

Online Resource for Indiana
Check out the Indiana Morels & Mushrooms Message Board at: *www.morels.com/indiana*

Ohio

No festivals are listed for this state.

Online Resource for Ohio
Check out the Ohio Mushroom Society's web page at *www.ohiomushroom.org* or the Ohio Morels & Mushrooms Message Board at *www.morels.com/ohio*

Minnesota

While this state has superb hunting opportunities for morels, no major festivals were found for this state. However, it should be noted that not only has the yellow morel mushroom (*Morchella esculenta*) been designated the official fungus of the state, Minnesota was the only state to select an official state fungus at the time that the state legislature designated it in 1984!

Online Resource for Minnesota
Check out the Minnesota Morels & Mushrooms Message Board at *www.morels. com/minnesota*

Pennsylvania

No festivals are listed for this state.

Online Resource for Pennsylvania
Check out the Pennsylvnia Morels and Mushroom Message Board at *www.morels.com/pennsylvania*

New York

No festivals are listed for this state.

Online Resource for New York
Check out the New York Morels and Mushroom Message Board at *www.morels.com/newyork*

CPSIA information can be obtained
at www.ICGtesting.com
Printed in the USA
LVHW010928050422
715337LV00008B/315